The Geriatric Sex Guide

Written and Illustrated By:
Dixie

Published in the U.S. © 1991 by
Ivory Tower Publishing Company, Inc.

Manufactured in the United States of America

30 29 28 27 26 25 24 23 22 21 20 19 18 17 16 15 14 13 12 11 10 9 8 7 6 5 4 3

Ivory Tower Publishing Co., Inc.
125 Walnut St., Watertown, MA 02172
Telephone #: (617) 923-1111 Fax #: (617) 923-8839

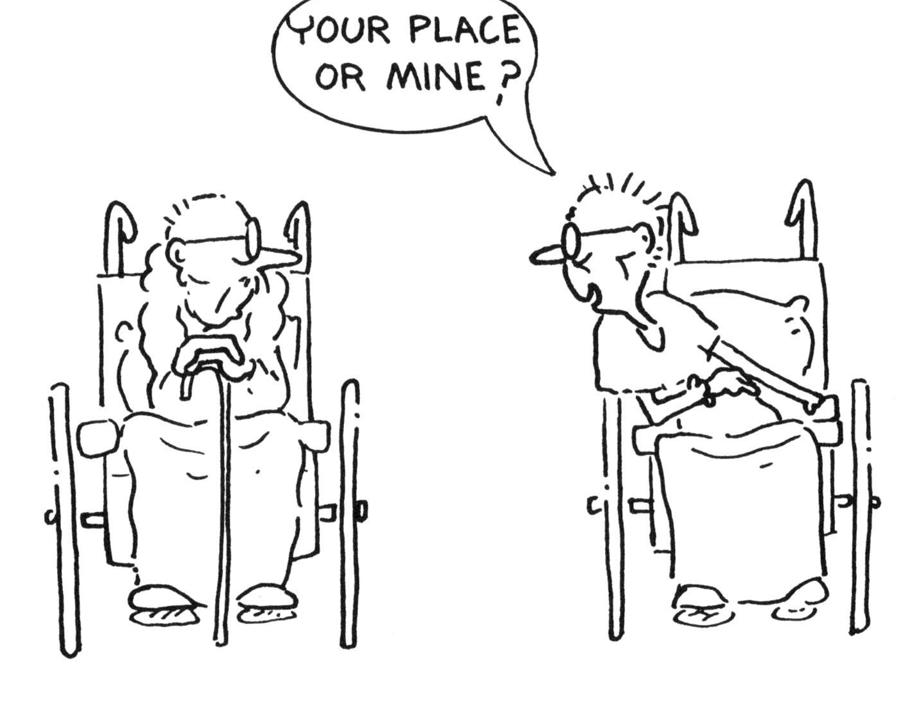
YOUR PLACE OR MINE?

WELL VICAR, YOUR CHARMING YOUNG WIFE HAS CERTAINLY MADE AN IMPRESSION ON MY GEORGE!

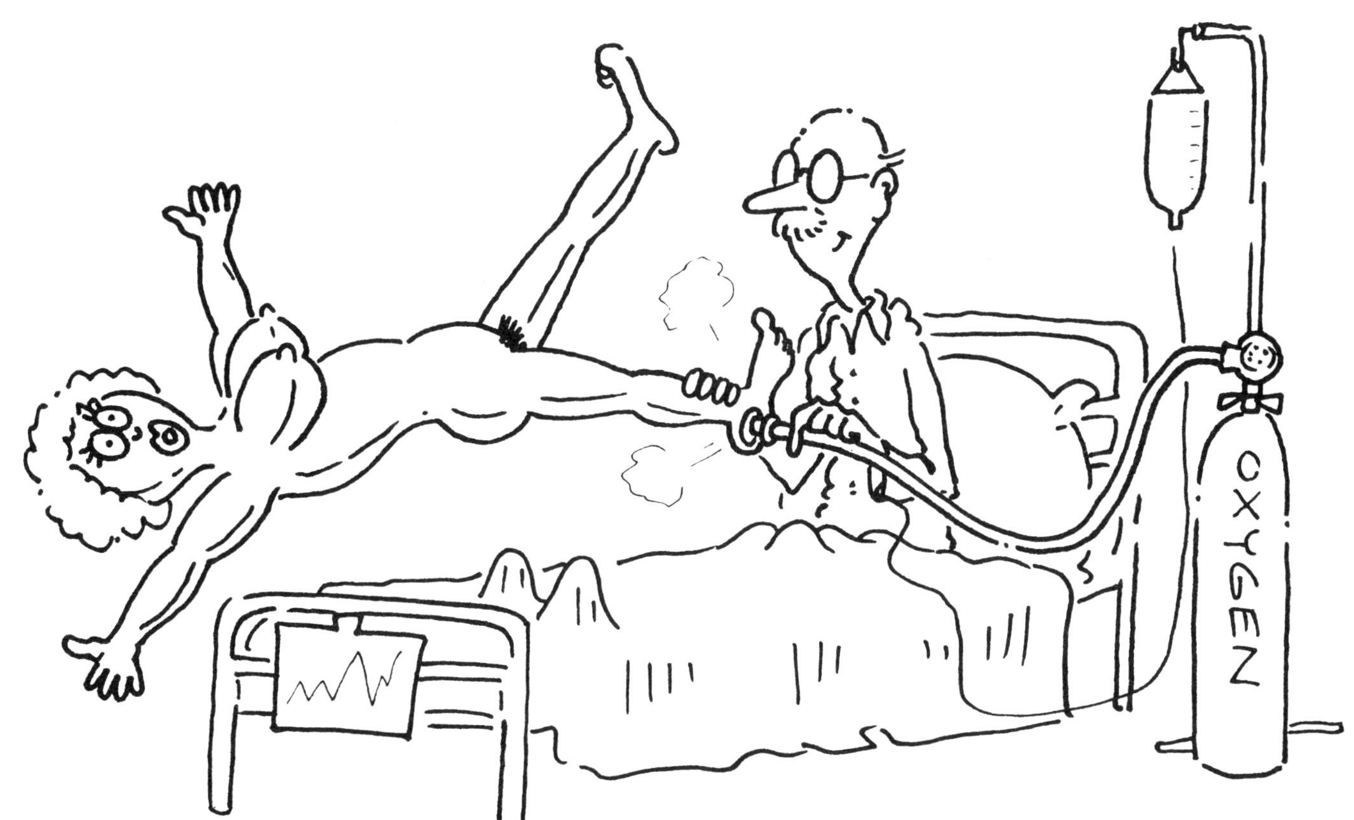
OXYGEN

HOW TO
69
?

OXYG

I LIKE HISTORICAL FILMS!

SEX CINEMA

NOW SHOWING!

SEXY SCHOOLGIRLS!

MAN
WANTED
FOR
SEX
ATTACKS
HE SAYS HE'S COME ABOUT THE JOB!

YOU'LL FEEL A LITTLE PRICK... BUT WHY CHANGE THE HABIT OF A LIFETIME ?

BRAGGING AGAIN?

OF COURSE GEORGE IS BASICALLY VERY SHY!

I DON'T LIKE THE PILL... IT KEEPS ROLLING OUT!

WHO SAID ALL MEN ARE EQUAL?

NUDIST
BEACH

TOPLESS
BEACH

I SAID..I'VE HEARD THAT TOO MUCH SEX STUNTS YOUR GROWTH!

YES, OF COURSE I REMEMBER, ..NO..DON'T TELL ME, I NEVER FORGET A FACE!..

NUDIST BEACH

OF COURSE SIZE DOESN'T MATTER ... WHAT MAKES YOU THINK THAT STUMPY?

THANK YOU
BLIND

FANCY A STIFF ONE?

ICE CREAM
CRUSHED NUTS SIR ?
NO...ARTHRITIS!

I'M IN THE MOOD NOW... BUT BY THE TIME WE'RE NAKED I WON'T BE!

NO..."DROP YER DRAWERS" AREN'T THE THREE LITTLE WORDS I HAD IN MIND!

BREATHTAKING VIEW ISN'T IT GEORGE?

BLESS YOU!

THAT'S NOT QUITE WHAT I MEANT ABOUT MORE FUN IN BED!

COAL

BE GENTLE WITH ME!

DON'T BE SILLY
DEAR...IT'S
PROBABLY
RIGORMORTIS!

OF COURSE I STILL CHASE WOMEN... TROUBLE IS... I CAN'T REMEMBER WHY!

WHAT I REALLY MISS
IS THE OLD
WHAM BAM
THANK YOU
MAAM!

DID THE EARTH MOVE FOR YOU TOO ALBERT?

HOW MANY TIMES HAVE I TOLD YOU ABOUT MAKING THIS BED PROPERLY... LOOK WHAT I'VE JUST FOUND IN IT!

HE'S ALWAYS BEEN THE INQUISITIVE TYPE!

WELL, ACCORDING TO THIS... A GOOD BLOW JOB WILL DO THE TRICK!
JOY OF SEX

OF COURSE I'VE JUST FARTED... YOU DON'T THINK I ALWAYS SMELL LIKE THIS DO YOU?

I'VE BEEN HAPPILY MARRIED FOR TEN YEARS....OUT OF OVER FORTY THAT IS!

IT'S NOT YOUR MIND THAT NEEDS EXPANDING!
JUNG
FREUD

LOOK... YOU CHOSE YOUR HOT WATER BOTTLE...

"HAPPY?...I'LL SAY!... I CAUGHT 'ER BETWEEN HEADACHES, LAST NIGHT!"

"THAT'S ALL YOU THINK ABOUT.....

.....SEX AND BLOODY FOOTBALL!"

"BERT'S ALWAYS BEEN A BIT OF A LADIES MAN......CAN'T SEE IT MYSELF, THOUGH!"

"AND WHAT HAVE YOU TWO BEEN UP TO WHILE WE WERE OUT?"

40-
20-
30-

"WHY SHOULDN'T IT BE MICHAEL JACKSON IN DISGUISE ?"

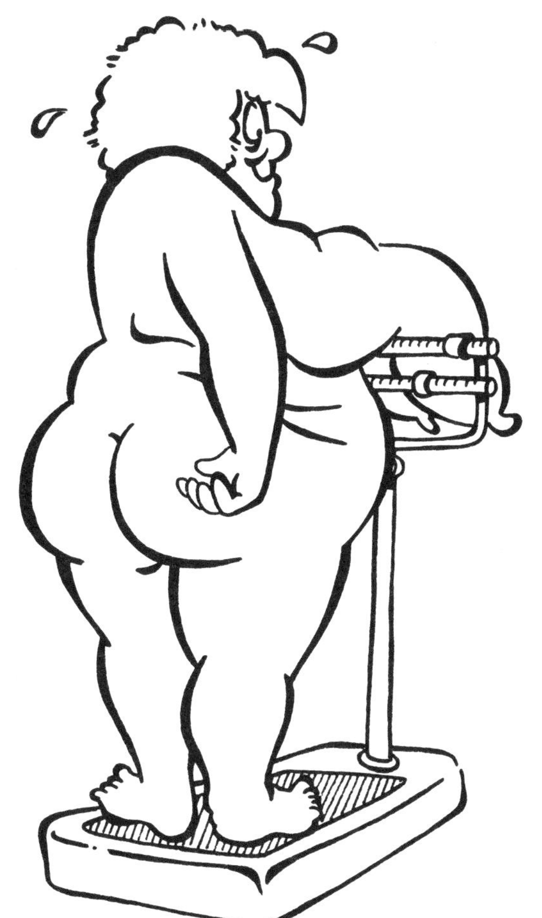

"OF COURSE I STILL RESPECT YOU...... I JUST DON'T RECOGNIZE YOU!"

"SECOND OPINION?...SURE!..YOU'VE GOT A TINY PRICK TOO!"

"HE'S VERY PROUD OF HIS WORLD WAR ONE SHRAPNEL SCAR!"

"SHE'S GOTTA HAVE A VERY LOW SEX DRIVE OR A VERY GOOD SENSE OF HUMOR!"

"YES.. IT'S OUR FIRST TIME TOO!"

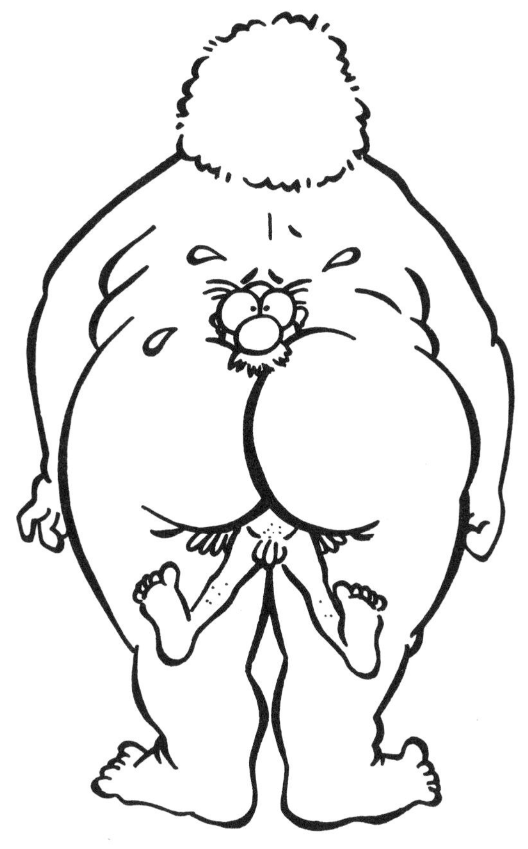

"GEORGE?.....GEORGE!?"

"...OR TO PUT IT ANOTHER WAY, IT'S JUST UNDER 50¢ A POUND!"

"FER GAWD'S SAKE, WOMAN...WILL YOU PLEASE STOP FARTIN'?"

"69?....IF YOU THINK I'M ***COOKING*** THIS TIME OF NIGHT...."

"I'VE ALREADY GIVEN!"

" I'D LOVE TO GET INTO YOUR DRAWERS! "

" OOH!... IS THAT 'COZ YOU LOVE ME? "

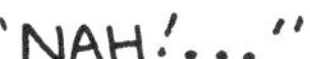

"NAH!..."

"...I'VE JUST CRAPPED IN MINE!"

"FIVE BUCKS USED TO BUY MORE THAN A KICK IN THE NUTS!"

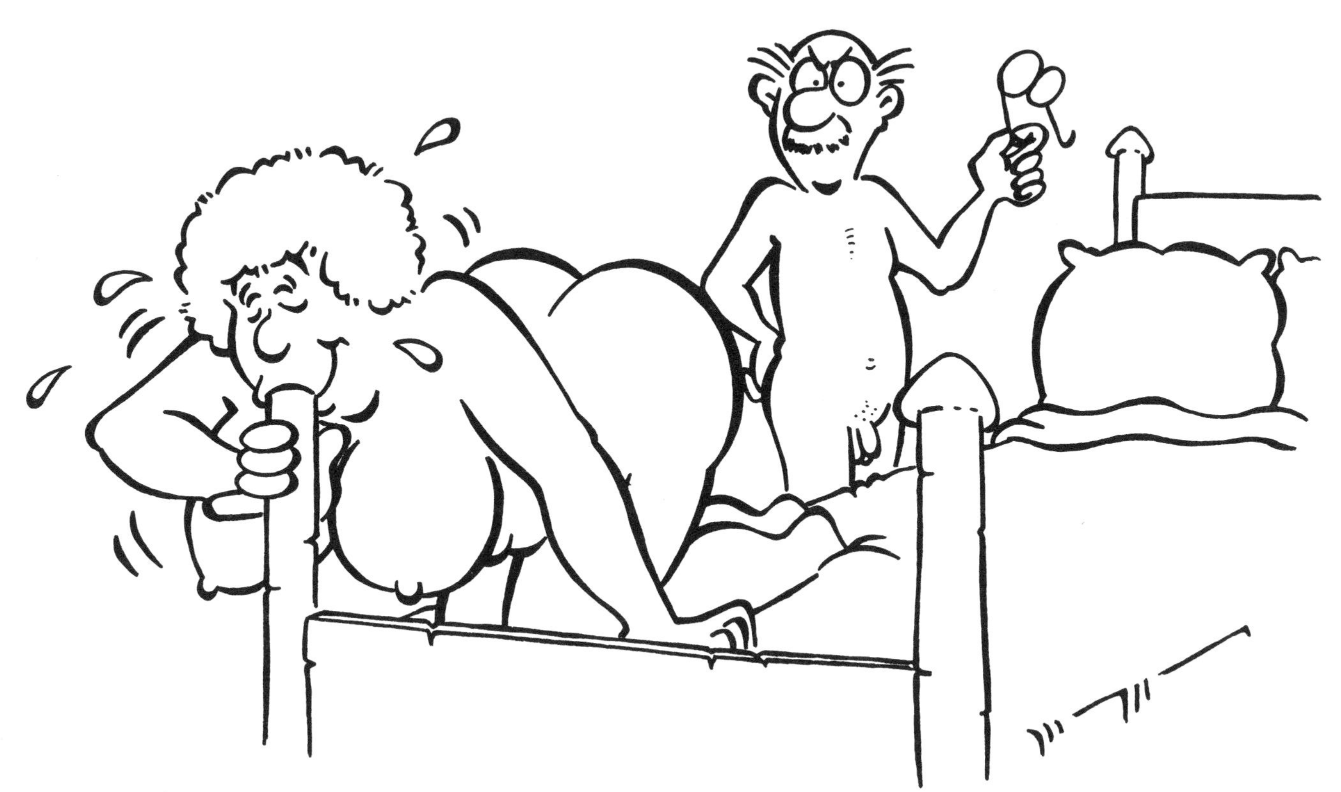

"FER GAWD'S SAKE, WOMAN!...PUT YER GLASSES ON!"

"NO! YOU DEAF OLD BAT! . . . . . I DIDN'T SAY *FLORAL* SEX!"

"ARE YOU SURE YOU DIDN'T MARRY ME JUST FOR MY MONEY, JOSIE?"

"LOOK AT THE SIZE OF *HIM!*...OOH! HE'S GOING TO DO IT *AGAIN!*...AND LOOK AT THE KNOB ON *THAT* ONE!..."

SELF
RAISING
FLOUR

" OF COURSE I LOVE YER . . . . . I FUCK YER, DON'T I ? "

"IS THE HONEYMOON OVER, OR IS IT JUST MY NOSE?"

"HE'S ALWAYS BEEN A BIT OF A TIT-MAN!"

"DAMN IT! . . . MY NUTS HAVE FALLEN OFF!"

" STOP SHOWIN' OFF, GEORGE ! "

"I THINK GRANDAD'S TAKEN A FANCY TO YOU!"

"CAN'T WAIT TO HEAR THE STORY BEHIND THIS ONE, EH, NURSE?"

"I TOLD YOU A MINI SKIRT WOULD LOOK STUPID, DIDN'T I?"

"OH, GO ON, MRS. GRABBITT...A BIT O' COCK-SUCKIN' NEVER HURT ANYBODY!"

"THAT REMINDS ME.....HOW'S YOUR HUSBAND?"

"SO WHAT?..I'VE GOT A STIFF NECK... BUT I DON'T GO SHOWING *THAT* TO EVERYBODY!"

"HOW CAN YOU FILL ME WITH HAPPINESS WITH A TWO-INCH DICK?"

"HELLO...GUINNESS BOOK OF RECORDS?..."

"ARE YOU *SURE* THIS'LL CURE MY TONSILITIS?"

"IT MAY BE GOOD FOR YOUR TENSION...BUT IT DOES NOTHING FOR MY ARTHRITIS!"

" DON'T MISS A SINGLE BLOODY TRICK, DO YOU ? "

IT'S THE WIFE'S IDEA... I CAME OUT WITHOUT A SCARF YESTERDAY... AND GOT A STIFF NECK!